Common Sense 2.0

Restoring our Culture's Foundation

Jim Dickson

Common Sense 2.0

Restoring our Culture's Foundation

Cover design based on an Unsplash image by
Samuel Branch
unsplash.com/photos/ZPVisr0s_hQ

Grateful for the publishing services provided by
DwightClough.com

Paperback ISBN: 9798361691623

Table of Contents

Preface

A lifetime interest in American history and government has led in the past three years to writing a series of six commentaries[1] to answer the question, "What is going on and what can we do about it?" Each commentary answered one question but opened the door to another, and then another, and another.

The last commentary, *On Fire for God Handbook*, was written to be a resource for leaders to change the world, where God had placed them, from man's way to God's way. What is still needed is the strong message contained in an old hymn, "Rise up o men of God, have done with lesser things."

[1] Available from Amazon: *Mere Humanity*—Jim Dickson. Profits go to Ukrainian relief.

This commentary is designed to be that strong message. The "lesser things" include excess power, prosperity, and pleasure[2]—material attractions of the world that have addictive tendencies that can distract well-meaning citizens from making spiritual values the cornerstone of their lives. This is a nation-wide problem that is leading to loss of freedom as significant as that faced by the Founders under the King of England.

This commentary is designed to be a wake-up call not unlike that of Thomas Paine's book Common Sense in 1776 which is generally felt to be one of the most significant factors in uniting the colonies to declare independence from what was at that time the greatest nation in the world.

---

[2] For practical purpose in this writing these three tendencies are used to serve as illustrations of dozens of attractions that can lead to addiction. For example Goggle lists more than 15 types of 12-Step-Programs.

In writing this commentary it was clear that:

- There was a correlation between the situation faced by the Founding Fathers in 1776 and the present condition of our country.

- The King was the enemy then, but that the enemy today is hidden in hearts, in hearts in need of cleansing.[3]

Paine clearly communicated his message in the opening sentence of an article he wrote December 23, 1776 to the colonists who were facing a desperate winter he wrote.

"These are the times that try men's souls. The summer soldier and the sunshine patriot will, in this crisis shrink from the service of their country; but he that stands it now,

---

[3] Blessed are the pure in heart, for they shall see God. Matthew 5:8

deserves the love and thanks of man and woman."

The same message is needed today: These are times that try men's souls. We don't need summer soldiers and sunshine patriots; he that stands now "deserves the love and thanks of man and woman."

To gain clarity in writing, the author's decision to re-read Paine's book Common Sense was wise. An added gift was to read it from the 2012 Penguin Books edition with Introductions by Richard Beeman, especially his brief but very helpful biography of Thomas Paine. This commentary contains a number of references from that publication.

Background

Common Sense 2.0 is designed to provide a clear understanding of where we came from and where we are going. This requires going back to creation.

Our Founding Fathers believed in a Creator, and the Creator as God as evident in the preamble to the Declaration of Independence.[4] The Creator gave man, you and me, dominion over his creation and clearly stated man was made in the image of God. In the Garden of Eden Adam, the first man, chose to go his own way and acquired a sin nature. As descendants of Adam, there is a

---

[4] "We hold these truths to be self-evident, that all men are *created* equal, that they are endowed by their *Creator* with certain unalienable Rights…" with a preface, "the separate and equal station to which the *Laws of Nature and of Nature's God* entitle them…

battle between good and evil going on within each us, as well as a potential battle with every one of Adam's descendants—everyone!

This writing is based on the understanding that we are made in the image of God so that we choose to live God's way, but have a sin nature constantly seeking to go man's way.

Man's way leads to loneliness and *anxiety*. It is rather amazing that:

> *A medical advisory group to the federal government has recommended that all adult Americans age 19-64 be screened for anxiety. Earlier this year the U.S, Preventive Services Task Force which advises both the Department of Health and Human Services and*

A better study would be the teachings in Genesis chapter 1 where the conflict between man's image of God and man's sin nature began and is still a major cause of anxiety.

We all have a soul that ultimately decides which way we will go, God's way or man's way. That largely depends on whether we are feeding our *spiritual* nature or our *sin* nature. Our spiritual nature involves *values* such as honesty, purity, gentleness, self-control, patience, and thoughtfulness. Our sin nature involves an unhealthy love for materialism.

The Creator provided an instruction book that contains teachings to keep us on his path including The Greatest Commandment to love God and neigh-

---

[5] Wall Street Journal, 09/28/2022 p. A15

bors, the Ten Commandments, and The Beatitudes with his plan for happiness. The latter also includes a promise, "blessed are the pure in heart for they shall see God,"[6] to enable us to know God's plan in so far as our hearts are pure.

Common sense tells us that if we don't follow instruction of the one who created us there will be trouble. However the institutions of our culture, except for religious organizations, not only don't teach these instructions but they have a bias against them as we shall see later. This was opposite of the intent of the Founders. In 240 years we have walked away from God's plan so that man's way largely prevails.[7] The result is

[6] Matthew 5:8

[7] This should not be surprising. For example a child could go through a public education system 5 hours/day 180 days/year for 12 years (10,000+ hours) without hearing the word "God".

12

a culture today in which works of the flesh prevail.[8]

The intent of Common Sense 2.0 is to restore the spiritual foundation of our nation. That requires we:

1. Recognize we are in a war against a tyrant,

2. Acknowledge the battle is between our image of God and our fallen nature,

3. Emphasize "society" and minimize government,

4. Admit the need for soul cleansing to see God's will clearly,

5. Be in a support group for accountability, and

---

[8] "The acts of the flesh are obvious: sexual immorality, impurity and debauchery; idolatry and witchcraft; hatred, discord, jealousy, fits of rage, selfish ambition, dissensions, factions and envy; drunkenness, orgies, and the like. I warn you, as I did before, that those who live like this will not inherit the kingdom of God." Galatians 5:19-20

6. Join with others to transform cultural institutions

War against a tyrant

America you are precariously close to losing your freedom, the freedom received at creation when man was made in the image of God, the freedom our Founders fought for 240 years ago, and the freedom Lincoln reaffirmed 80 years later stating, "This nation under God shall have a new birth of freedom."

Freedom is a precious heritage. We hold it in trust to pass on to future generations. Why are we losing freedom? Because…

We have gone from being a nation with spiritual *values* to a secular culture with addictive material *tendencies* such as excess power, pleasure and prosperity[9] that are devoid of values. A recent oft-quoted survey reveals that two decades ago 70% of Americans belonged to a church, mosque or synagogue; today fewer than half feed on spiritual food. What we eat determines what we become and we have been feeding on secular food largely provided by the TV, newspapers, radio, social media, and movies rather than spiritual sources that teach values. *Spiritual values satisfy*, secular *materialism* only *satisfies momentarily*, then leads to a never-ending addictive quest for more.

The evidence is everywhere. Robert R. Reilly affirms,

---

[9] For practical purpose in this writing these three tendencies are used to serve as illustrations of dozens of attractions that can lead to addiction. For example Goggle lists more than 15 types of 12-Step-Programs.

The virtue needed to sustain the republic is fast disappearing.[10] Violence, anger, loneliness, and hate increase while love for God and neighbors decreases. The 200 year emphasis by the Founder's on "We the People" has turned into a nation of individuals seeking fulfillment in self-centered me-ism. We were created for greatness but our addictions have become a stranglehold on our "image of God" goodness. In regard to freedom we are committing mass suicide.

Reilly's book provides another significant contribution on the intent of the Founders regarding *the laws of nature and*

---

[10] Robert R. Reilly, America on Trial, Ignatius 2006, p. 323. His Epilogue details the growth of historicity beginning in the 1920s as a strong factor in erasing the moral authority of the Founders.

nature's God.[11] Reilly warns of the danger of human standards,

> *As soon as one moves from the rational 'Laws of Nature and of Nature's God' to the one making human will that standard, one is headed for Leviathan. We are now enduring such a transformation in the United States where political rule is becoming increasingly arbitrary.*

The *laws of nature and nature's God* are not suggestions. They are mandates and God's standards for determining right and wrong, God's way or man's way. For this writing it is enough to summarize and select certain standards that flow from these laws.

Family—God made man in His image. He said "a man will leave his father and mother and be united to his wife,

---

[11] Declaration of Independence, paragraph 1

18

and they will become one flesh." He told the man and his wife to "Be fruitful and increase in number; fill the earth and subdue it."

Dominion—He gave man "dominion overall the earth" put man in "the Garden of Eden to work it and care for it."

Ten Commandments—No other Gods; no idols; no misuse of God's name; observe Sabbath; honor your Father and Mother; no murdering, adultery, stealing, giving false testimony, or coveting what belongs to others.

The Greatest Commandment—"Love the Lord your God with all your heart and with all your soul and with all your mind. This is the first and greatest commandment. And the second is like it: Love your neighbor as yourself."

Beatitudes—A call for a new attitude toward: the poor in spirit, those who mourn, the meek, those who hunger and thirst for righteousness; Be merciful; strive for purity; bless the peacemakers and those persecuted because of righteousness; Remember when people insult, persecute, and speak evil against you for my sake it is an opportunity to be blessed.

Caring—It is better to give than to receive. The Son of man came not to be served but to serve.

Sharing the Good News—Go make disciples of all nations…teaching them to observe all my commandments.

Are we staying with or straying from these standards? Among the many reasons this question is important is that numerous surveys show a close correlation between mental well-being and obedience. Just as we recognize the value of periodically checking on our physical

20

condition to assure our physical well-being the situation calls for periodic spiritual examinations.

This gives rise to a dilemma—we are often biased or blind to our personal spiritual faults but reluctant to involve others in discussing our inner feelings. This must change.

God's Commands

God's Plan provides a starting point for measuring spiritual health. Next is the need for following these standards both in regard to our culture and then in regard to our individual lives.

As for our culture, the greatest commandment says we are to love our neighbor as ourself. How are we doing on that? By far the media stories about everyday life and relationships are anything but loving. How often do we speak ill of other? Those with different political beliefs than ours? How often are our Presidents vilified by millions of citizens and by the media? Justified or not is not the point—speaking ill of others is not loving. Disagree yes, criticize yes, but speak the truth in love. God makes no exceptions to this command.

There are several reasons for this command. Hating is a stain on our culture, it is a work of the flesh, it adds to darkness, and it rarely if ever changes the other person. Hating government officials has the added negative of tearing down the house we all live in. This one command, "love your neighbor" if observed would have an immediate dramatic impact on restoring a spiritual culture.

How is our culture doing in regard to total love for God in the Greatest Commandment? One measurement is church membership. As cited earlier a recent survey showed that membership in a church, synagogue, or mosque had declined in just the last 20 years from 70% of the population to the mid-40s. That is not love for God. We are rapidly moving away from a culture focused on loving God.

Perhaps the biggest change in our culture's moving away from God relates to *family matters*. In the last twenty five years the judicial system has gone from labeling certain conduct illegal because it contradicted God's word to making it illegal to even suggest certain conduct is not right. Sexual behavior is a powerful force that cries out for open discussion and wisdom in decision making in changes that relate to God's plan. This has not been the case. A handful of un-elected judges has reversed moral practices without regard to consequences.

The net effect is the family unit is no longer a solid building block for raising up a generation imbued with values essential for spiritual growth. In its place we have rampant materialism that demeans. Family values are the glue that bond us as a nation and assures a constant flow of new generations that know right from wrong and live accordingly. Family values are the GPS that guides a culture upward. They are the balm that calms when threatened by turmoil. We must have leaders who will not tolerate disobedience to the *laws of nature and nature's God* and who will seek to purify our culture. Values must be taught in our families.

Cultural deterioration is the net result of individuals succumbing to our old nature's desire to "be like God". Formally this was primarily driven by individuals falling to the temptation of the tempter. Today this process has accelerated aided by social and commercial media, by an educational system that substitutes feeling for facts, and by government officials who pander to our human desire for power, prosperity, and pleasure.

Can we really improve on God's plan for genders? families? worship? civility?

caring? honesty? purity? serving? unselfishness? love?

Watch TV, read newspapers, go to movies and too often they trumpet the message of reprobate minds. Violence, greed, sex immorality, dishonesty, hate, anger, jealousy, idolatry, and on and on. Why do they do this? Greed! To make money. It is easier, faster and longer lasting to reach and stimulate the target audience by feeding man's old nature than by spending the time and effort required to communicate positive values. We need to be reminded of the need to be kind, good, admirable, lofty and energizing, values that raise a culture to the level where man who was made in the image of God was meant to live.

Consider three types of everyday communications. One is an appeal to man's lower nature, an easy but unhealthy way to get instant attention. Another is to focus on problems and issues of daily living. This is needed but mankind deserves more. A third is to ask questions and discuss matters that transcend daily living. Do you think what you are doing is what you were created to do? What would it take to make your life more meaningful? Enjoyable? Where do you think you will go when you die? How are you doing on loving your neighbors? Loving God?

Daily living man's way can be monotonous and lead to boredom and loneliness, paths that lead to a search for short term excitement and too often on to addiction. As previously discussed under Beatitudes, God's plan is for joy and happiness that is lasting. That calls for obedience.

Obedience

Obedience to God's commands today borders on *disobedience* which is so widespread it is easy to forget why obedience is important; it is the path to love and to the fullness of God.

> *...and to know this love that surpasses knowledge—that you may be filled to the measure of all the fullness of Goa (Ephesians 3:19)*

The word "fullness" includes "abundance" and "overflowing." Our humanness is immediately inclined to think of material wealth, but the biblical passage is concerned with spiritual blessings such as love, joy, peace and self-control. It is hard to think of any of the spiritual concerns people have today, including anxiety, that wouldn't find relief through obedience. Here is why.

Anxiety is a by-product of the battle going on in each of us between the image of God implanted in us at creation and our sin nature. If God had given us his spirit we would all be gods so he wisely just gave us his image. As discussed later in the chapter *Seek Higher Power* an image doesn't have the power to override our old nature. However Holy Spirit power is available for the asking but it takes a high level of obedience to say no to self and allow God's power to fight the battle for us. His spirit gives life to God's image when we seek his help.

Perhaps the greatest blessing from obedience is eternal life. In that widely publicized John 3:16 passage scripture teaches that eternal life is a gift from belief in Jesus. Man's way however is often a widespread misconception that heaven is a given for living a good life. With few exceptions popular theology discourages talk about the eternal life. This is a matter of such extreme importance that it deserves high priority in the thinking of believers. It will take leaders on fire for God to make this a priority.

One difficulty to scriptural teachings on eternal life is the simplicity of the transaction. It can be as easy as, "Lord I believe you are the son of God. I need help. Take over my life and make me what I was intended to be." It sounds too good to be true. Nonetheless all that is required is to trade our way for God's way, garbage for glory.

The daily rewards for *obedience* to God's Word are immense. On the other hand the payback for *disobedience* is beyond what words can describe and not a subject that requires examination.

A final word regarding obedience. The Old Testament/Hebrew Bible is a filled with examples of retribution for disobedience. Today some people feel the New Testament brings God's love in a way that there will be no more retribution. Not true. For example Acts 5:1-10 tells the story of Ananias and Sapphira. They sold property but "lied to men" and "kept for yourself some of the money you received." Both "fell down and died" and "great fear seized the whole church and all who heard about these things."

Jesus said, "Do not think that I have come to abolish the Law or the Prophets; I have not come to abolish them but to fulfill them. Matthew 5:17" A new level of obedience is required.

Founders' Contribution

There is no greater source for us to understand the importance of God's plan than to reflect on the Founding Father's understanding of this matter. A review of the founding of our nation and the vision of the Founders in entrusting it to us enables us to see God's plan for today more clearly.

In 1774 there was a meeting of two men with backgrounds so varied that the results of that visit could only be described as an act of God. One man was Thomas Paine whose father, a Quaker, was a tradesman with a son *reluctantly* following in that trade, off and on, for a number of years. Thomas had seven years of formal schooling. *Reluctance* included running away from home to enlist as a sailor only to be talked into coming back to the trade by his father. Later he did serve a brief stint as a sailor. There followed two marriages, one wife dying "tragically with her death the following year;" a stint as an excise collector but suspended for not doing the work, time in taverns and coffee houses, and writing petitions. The latter revealed that despite no job and a poor work record he had an ability to write clearly and logically that was to be his forte.

The other man was Benjamin Franklin, 31 years older than Paine. Franklin also started as a tradesman (printer), but then owned his own shop, became prominent in writing, and gained fame as a renowned experimental scientist, an influential American colonial agent, and a Founding Father. He was in

England in 1774 to represent the colonial government.

Paine's experience his first 30 years left him with deep-seated anger about the fairness of life in England. He decided to go to America. Before leaving he arranged for a visit with Franklin. Paine received a letter of introduction addressed to Franklin's son-in-law in Philadelphia saying "I think him very capable" and recommending Paine be given consideration for employment. The letter was at that time a high point in Paine's seedy life and served to open doors in high places for him in America.

In the course of history the meeting and letter made it possible for Paine to use his latent writing ability to write a 47 page book, *Common Sense*.

The book was designed to persuade the colonists that their cause was not the affair of a city, province, or kingdom, but of a continent, and an opportunity "to form the noblest, purest constitution on the face of the earth" that would "effect humanity to the end of time."[12] These were persuasive and prophetic words for which he has not been given enough credit due to later events in his life.[13] He had an intuitive sense of the importance of individuals, of freedom, and the fallacy of birthright.

Paine's *Common Sense* was a stirring argument denouncing the whole concept of hereditary monarchy and the distinc-

---

[12] Specific details of Paine's life are from the 20212 book "Common Sense", Penguin Books edition and primarily from the introduction by Richard Beeman pp. xxii-xxv.

[13] Paine's early writings encouraging independence relied on the Bible. Later he lost belief in Christ and was scorned by the colonists. Only a handful people came to his burial in New Rochelle, N.Y. A 1995 edition of *Common Sense* published by Barnes & Noble, Gregory Tietjen states Paine's bones where dug up in 1819, possibly taken to England but are now lost.

tion between kings and subjects. The issue, said Paine, is freedom.

Paine had a keen insight on the roles of *society*[14] and *government*, an insight that greatly needs to be understood today. He said society is produced by our wants, promotes happiness, unites our affections, encourages interaction, and is a benefactor. In short, enables us to enjoy our freedom. Government, on the other hand, is only necessary because of our wickedness, functions negatively, creates distinctions and is a punisher. (He did realize that government is a necessary evil to throttle our freedom when our old nature leads us to sin.)

Common Sense changed the mindset of the colonists and their leaders from "We must compromise" with the king to

[14] Defined as: "The conventions and opinions of a like-minded group." These grew rapidly after independence when people began to realize that they, not the king, needed to take responsibility for their welfare.

"The time has come for us to take responsibility for ourselves, to declare independence, and leave the mother country."

Paine's reasoning in Common Sense gave the Founding Fathers the confidence needed to declare independence from England, knowing that was the will of the majority of the colonists.

Paine taught that the king was a tyrant who provided security at the price of loss of freedom. For the colonists this was a huge step in their thinking but not unlike, other than in size, the step every individual makes in leaving home.

Our Culture Today

How does the Paine's experience apply to our culture today? In 1787 at the signing of the Constitution Franklin is quoted as saying, "You have a republic if you can keep it." Franklin knew human nature. He knew it would be difficult for people who had known the security of a king but then had to fight seven years to gain freedom now had to realize they would still need to fight a battle, this time against their sin nature's desire to do what it wanted to do.

This concern of Franklin's is our issue today. In its simplest sense do we do *what is right* or do we do what our sin nature *feels* is right. The former is determined by our Constitution, legislation, court interpretations, and spiritual and cultural values. The latter by our subjective self.

The Founding Fathers had a strong spiritual bias. The Declaration of Independence states all men are *created* equal and endowed by their *creator* with certain unalienable rights. They believed in a creator who gave birth to heaven and earth and all who dwell therein. They believed in "the laws of nature and of nature's God". They believed in God's way.

Man's way on the other hand is a slippery slope. How we *feel* as an individual about a matter is often stronger than what we *think*. That is compounded by the reality that each of us is working from a different data base based on background and experience. Feeling may seem to be important but it is a weak leg to stand on in decision making.

The input for decisions made on the basis of subjective *feelings* as to what is right, or decisions made on the basis of objective *facts* as to what is right is made clear in scripture. To make right decisions requires a higher power to override our sin nature. Decisions made on the basis of *feeling* lead to works of the flesh including anger, hate, immorality, impurity, selfishness, violence, "and the like". Decisions made on the basis of *facts* flow from the work of the Holy Spirit and lead to love, joy, peace, kindness, goodness and more.[15]

Today we are a culture with a strong emphasis on *feeling,* man's way. It is not surprising we are a culture in disarray. The vast majority of media sources and their stories of daily events reflect works of the flesh rather than fruit of the spirit. A brief look at the last 100 years, if one is open to accepting generalities, is help-

---

[15] Galatians 5:19-20 & 22-23

ful in revealing how we got to our present state of affairs.

The roaring 1920s were a time to let loose after World War I; pleasure and prosperity were widespread.

Not surprisingly a Great Depression in the 1930s followed. Was this the Creator's retribution for waywardness? It was difficult but a time of turning to God for help.

WW II in the 1940s united the country both in work effort and spirituality with weekly worship and turning to God, especially in battle, the norm.

The Eisenhower years of the 1950s, after the Great Depression and WW II, were a time to get on with daily living, raise a family, work hard, and continue with church[16] life. One big problem, much of church life was on the surface— enough belief for comfort but not enough for life changes. Revivals and campus ministries began and flourished but, to use the words of Elton Trueblood, churches offered "mild Christianity."

A major change, not necessarily for good, began in the 1960s. The generations who came out of the Great Depression and WW II were in general satisfied just to get on with daily living. The post WW II generation wanted more, wanted change, wanted to express their feelings in their lifestyle, music, movies, and more. Self-control to their parents meant obedience to established

---

[16] For simplicity the words worship and church are used in this writing to refer to churches, mosques, and synagogues and their respective religious activity in the United States

42

norms; self-control to the next generation meant "I will control what my 'self' wants."

Let's pause in chronology to reflect on a subtle but exceedingly significant action. In the '60s there was a well-meaning concern for the poor, culminating in a government program that came to be known as "The Great Society." It was an ambitious series of policies proposed by President Lyndon Johnson to help the needy. The Great Society contradicted what Thomas Paine said 200 years earlier, that "society" and "government" should not be combined as the former was good, the latter bad. Combining "society" and "government", like mixing black and white paint, was a mistake. The objective was good, the solution was bad.

Combining "society" and "government," into one government agency created a number of major problems. One, politicians can't resist using programs as a vote-getter, never get rid of it and keep making it bigger. Two, a traditional concern for needy "family and friends" was assigned to semi-professional and professional government agencies that could never provide the personal touch needed in dealing with humanitarian needs.[17] Finally, from that time on to the present it is no over-statement to say that the populace now looks primarily to the government as the care-giver for those in need.

By combining "society" and "government" and not following Paine's wisdom the country is going down the path of socialism as a central concept of the United States government. Since 1970s the Great Society bent toward socialism has continued to grow for 50 years and

---

[17] By contrast, in the 1930s my parents had 10-12 different needy individuals or families come to live with us (on the farm) for days and weeks and one family for 15 months. This was not uncommon and my wife and I repeated this practice for the first 20 years of our marriage.

44

shows no signs of changing, even becoming more all-encompassing. e.g. Student loan forgiveness, free school lunches for everyone, proposed anxiety screening and on and on.

Why is this not a good idea? While this is the subject for another writing suffice it to say socialism discourages individual creativity, resourcefulness, responsibility, and ultimately destroys freedom with China, Russia, Cuba, and North Korea as prime examples. Freedom that arises out of spiritual values stimulates individuals to be a resource for goodness. Socialism communicates a message that if I don't, someone else will. Socialism is secular materialism on a grand scale, materialism that is devoid of values and can only provide fulfillment temporarily and then the search for something that satisfies starts all over again.

Values

Spirituality is crucial. It gives birth to values, values that transcend the routine of everyday living. Deep inside each person is an empty space in a soul that hungers for a relationship with its creator. *Spiritual starvation* and loss of values is a major cause of the unrest, violence, and anger in our culture today.

Many of the early colonists came for religious purposes. They brought an abundance of spiritual values that, like money in the bank, served as a significant support for the nation for two centuries. It has been used up. Franklin's warning that "You have a republic if you can keep it" is now being revealed as prophetic.

Thomas E. Ricks Pulitzer Prize winning book *First Principles*[18] is a scholarly study of what America's Founders learned about values, especially from ancient Greeks and Roman leaders. Several quotes are pertinent to our situation today. (italics added)

> *"John Adam wrote in a letter to his wife, The new government… will require a Purification from our Vices, and an Augmentation of our Virtues or they will be no Blessings,"*

> *"Washington built into his life the qualities of honesty, patriotism, and self-sacrifice" based on Cato, a 2nd century B.C. Roman leader.*

> *"The conspiracies of Catiline and Caesar against the liberty of their*

____

[18] Thomas E Ricks, First Principles, HarperCollins books, 2020

Note the Founder's emphasis: purification, virtues, honesty, patriotism, self-sacrifice followed by the understanding that love of luxury leads to corruption.

Materialism, secular living, has no values worthy of the name and leaves us plodding along with an inner battle going on between our "image of God" nature and our self-centered sin nature. The battle results in frustration, anger, and violence. But the problem gets worse. There are few watchmen on the wall today to warn of the impending danger.

A gradual *walking away from goodness* is pervasive in our culture. Many of those strong in their spiritual life who should be leading the charge are unknowingly being neutralized by excess power, prosperity, and pleasure. Elton Trueblood's mild Christianity of the '60s is even milder today.

Your author had this experience. After working with my wife in ministry for 30 years in the area of discipleship and evangelism, I had a (minor) bout of Covid. This was followed by an epiphany, an awakening, and I came to realize I had been "walking away from goodness." I was spending too many hours a day on trivia, things I knew were not fulfilling and things that distracted from the responsibility the Creator has given to all mankind. I had let pleasure and prosperity become too important in my life. Then I looked at other believers and saw similar distractions which raised the question, "Where are the watchman on the wall?" The awakening led to writing this commentary.

One measure of *"walking away from goodness"* is in the previous cited surveys that show church attendance in the

United States has decreased from about 70% of the population to the mid-40s (in the 20 years before Covid). Today's irregular church attendance is counter to God's command to "forsake not the assembling of ourselves together." Hebrew 10:25 raises the larger question of whether people today have neglected other forms of spiritual feeding including prayer, Bible study, quiet time, and fellowship.

Why the catastrophic reduction in church attendance? A major cause relates to not realizing the importance of values in daily life, especially *self-control* and *love*.

The name *self-control* is no coincidence. We have a "self" whose nature is to create problems that needs to be *controlled*. The Creator knew Adam would be tempted to go his own way and he included self-control in the fruit of his Spirit.[19] Unfortunately self-control be-

---

[19] Galatians 5:22-23

50

came a low priority for man in one of the areas where it is most needed, sexual relations. With the development of birth control pills in the 1960s, a key part of God's plan for man's maturing process, self-control in sexual matters, has been largely abandoned.

The other especially significant value is *love* which has the unique ability to hide a multitude of sins[20] and has the stature of the "Greatest Commandment" upon which "all the law and the prophets depend"[21]. *Love* ties the Old Testament (the Hebrew Bible) together with the New Testament in one story of God's plan for man. If we would love God, who has a plan for each individual, and love our neighbor as ourself, all mankind would be joined together in one world, loving God, enjoying him forever, and caring for one another.

---

[20] James 5:20

[21] Matthew 22:16-20

This will require a new type of man, free from the power of addictive tendencies.

Addictive Tendencies

Our old nature is loaded with addictive tendencies. (re-read that sentence) Daily and hourly we are being lured by the world's emphasis on power, prosperity, and pleasure[22]: "I did it my way." "If it feels good do it." "You owe it to yourself." Sex, security or success are the bait in the majority of ads. A prosperous culture is full of folks that can be led down the path of man's ways, and also well-meaning people who can unknowingly be drawn away from spiritual values to man's ways.

A recent book review in the Wall Street Journal couldn't be more timely

---

[22] Balance is important. It is excess materialism that enables addictive tendencies to prevail.

and appropriate as an example of how widespread and shallow are our cultural addictive tendencies. The article is a review of the book, *The Quest for Wellness.*[23] One quote from the book discusses "cannabis-infused wellness weekends; of women eager to buy jade yoni eggs, therapeutic crystals and chemical-free beauty products."

Quotes from the article:

G.K. Chesterton stated that people who choose not to believe in God will believe in anything…

Wellness has become an "aspirational obsession" for some and close to religious dogma for others."

The problem is that millions of Americans are looking to "wellness" to supply something it can't: refreshment in deep places that have

---

[23] WSJ, Sept. 21, 2022, A15 Authored by Rina Raphael and reviewed by Meghan Cox Gurdon

been left parched in the long, slow withdrawing of organized religion.

Two decades ago, 70% of Americans belonged to a church, mosque, or synagogue; today it's fewer than half.

The late David Foster Wallace noticed certain human propensities, "There is no such thing as not worshiping. Everybody worships."

Without religion people will believe anything. A people without religion searches frantically for "refreshment in the soul"…Everyone needs worships!

(Author's disclosure: I have never read any writing of the reviewer of this book and am quite sure the reviewer has not read anything I wrote.)

The article is just one of innumerable examples that reflect the state of the nation at this time for something "close to religious dogma."

If in reading the article you substitute for the word "wellness" any of the usual causes of addiction such as alcohol, tobacco, gambling, overeating, sex, and workaholic, you would basically be writing the same article and would come up with Rina Raphael's conclusions, especially "A people without religion searches frantically."

Like the alcoholic or any addict, typically there is a gradual walking away from goodness, lured by materialism. We are a people frantically searching for, but never finding, a substitute. We are a people being led by our sin nature into bondage. We are a people losing our freedom, a right the Founders named as a natural right of man.

Prepare to Act

What do we do now? Start by realizing addiction is a tyrant taking away our freedom.

Next do something. Thomas Paine did. He realized the Founders were in danger of losing their freedom so he wrote the pamphlet *Common Sense* to warn the colonists. The pamphlet was widely read through-out the colonies and brought about a change in thinking from "compromise with the King" to "declare independence." Despite the hardships of a Valley Forge, the uncertainties relating 3-month military commitments, or the uncertainties of being paid, the colonists never lost their faith that they had en-

shrined in the declaration independence.[24] We need the same commitment
and belief.

Seek help. Without the aid of France
the colonists would not have been able
to win independence. Today we can
learn from Great Britain. As they dealt
with the passing of Queen Elizabeth II,
their monarch for seven decades, a great
outpouring of love emerged. The principles and values that the Queen exempli-
fied reminded the Brits that their culture
was embedded in values that flowed
from their Creator. The statement "we
shall see her again" was powerful. We received that same spiritual foundation
from our Founders and need to return
to it.

Institutions will be a major problem
in our battle for freedom today. Institu-

____

[24] "We hold these truth to be self-evident, that
all men are 'created' equal and endowed by
their 'creator' with certain unalienable rights…"

tions enable people with similar goals to work together. A key concern in the past twenty years is watchmen sleeping and not warning of institutions becoming bastions of humanism. K-12 schools, colleges, media, entertainment, and government at all levels now largely teach man's way, emphasizing feeling over facts and stressing wants rather than needs.

It is not always easy to change an individual's mind. It is very hard to change the collective minds of members of institutions but to restore freedom this must happen. Institutions must be infiltrated. This will require leaders on fire for God and it will require a return to God's plan for man as set out in God's instruction book, especially the Genesis chapters that set out the structure of the culture that has proven to be effective for several thousand years:

- Two genders[25], male and female determined biologically at birth.

- Marriage between a man and a woman with a lifetime commitment.

- Fruitful parents who "multiply."

- Children raised primarily by their parents, first at home and then in schools that reflect the values of the parents.

- A culture based on the Creator's plan including the Greatest Commandment to love God and your neighbor as yourself. The Ten Commandments providing guidance for right and wrong. The

---

[25] Affirmation of the traditional male/female roles is found in a recent wellness survey created by the Medical College of Wisconsin that covered 3 local counties. The survey found those living traditional male/female roles had significantly less anxiety and insecurity than those choosing alternate lifestyles.

Beatitudes[26] emphasizing happiness. The Sermon on the Mount to deal with practical aspects of everyday living.

How could we have abandoned the Creator's plan for our plan? Because as cited previously the majority of the culture no longer receives regular spiritual feeding even though God's instructions tells us to

consider how we may spur one another on toward love and good deeds, not giving up meeting together, as some are in the habit of doing, but encouraging one another.[27]

It is time to go on the attack. Several factors are relevant. Our battle is not against an army but an ideology.

---

[26] "Happiness of the highest kind" Chambers Concise English Dictionary 1991

[27] Hebrew 10:25-6

- Spiritual values are more powerful than secular beliefs.

- A small group of early Christians changed the culture of the powerful Roman Empire.

- Our Founders defeated the most powerful nation at that time in the world.

Thomas Paine laid out the arguments for the colonists to separate from England and said if you don't separate now the situation will only get worse. Similarly, now is the time to deal with our tyrant, our addictive tendencies, or the situation will only get worse. Spiritual power in you and me will prevail if we let this power control our lives.

Seek Higher Power

How do we defeat the tyrant? We can't. As descendants of Adam, the tyrant will always be in our genes. However there is help available to overpower and neutralize our addictive tendencies. Holy Spirit power is patiently waiting to bring fullness to the image of God in each one of us.

A simple way to receive Holy Spirit power is through prayer,

- Repent of addiction to the world's ways, the trivia, the excess power, prosperity, and pleasure that are distractions from God's ways.

- Ask the Holy Spirit to come into your life and control it.

- Thank him for making you who the person God created you to be.

Many people know the exact time and date when they received Holy Spirit power. Others just know their lives have changed from what they were to the power they are now experiencing. It is important to know the old ways no longer satisfy and need to be replaced by a "hunger and thirst for righteousness."

Receiving Holy Spirit is a key decision but it must not stop there. We must continually emphasize spiritual feeding including church attendance to worship, fellowship, prayer, quiet time, bible reading, study groups, outreach training, and service ministries. Without spiritual feeding our sin nature might re-emerge and be even more difficult to control.

How strong are we to be spiritually? Christ set the standard when he said *I came to cast fire upon the earth.*[28] That is strong. He made disciples on fire for God and then sent them out to make disciples of all nations.[29] The work of the twelve spread to change the culture of the Roman Empire. We will need this same fire and the same process, "train and send out."

John Wesley noted that "mild Christianity won't do it." He provided a model to make disciples on fire for God. His *Class Meetings* from 1740 to 1780 changed the culture of England when that country faced tyrant problems involving slavery and boys working long hours in factories and mines. Wesley's group members met weekly to share what God was doing in their lives with an emphasis on purity. The goal was

---

[28] Luke 12:49

[29] Matthew 28:18-20

heart cleansing.[30] God promises the pure in heart shall see God.[31]

Wesley's Class Meetings purified hearts so members could see God's plan for their lives. That is our goal if we are to preserve the freedom paid for by the Founders.

---

[30] See *John Wesley's Class Meetings*, D. Michael Henderson, Francis Asbury Press of Evangel Publishing House 1997

[31] "Blessed are the pure in heart for they shall see God".

Act!

The goal of Common Sense 2.0 is that of Thomas Paine, freedom from the tyrant. His tyrant was a King; our tyrant is our addictive tendencies that have lulled us into complacency. Materialism has replaced spirituality as the foundation of our nation. Materialism leads to works of the flesh and anxiety and loneliness; spirituality provides fruit of the spirit that include love, joy, faithfulness and self-control.

One historian, Isaac Kramnick, notes the United States owes its existence in part to the incendiary brilliance of Common Sense[32] because of the power with

---

[32] *Common Sense* published by Barnes & Noble, Gregory Tietjen, p. xv

which it infused the hearts of colonists with a desire for freedom. We need the same inspiration and commitment today, leaders and individuals rising up again to make God's ways the foundation of our country. This will require that churches and religious groups of all denominations, faith, and beliefs overlook their differences and come together for the high calling of freedom as did the extremely diverse colonists 240 years ago.

On Fire for God groups can come together to impact specific institutions such as education, media, and government that are leading the culture astray in harmful ways.

There are a growing number of examples nationally of schools, media, and governments being changed in this manner and there are numerous organizations to help with legal matters.

Think big, be sensitive to God's leading, and pray for divine intervention. God answered the colonists prayer at Yorktown when the French fleet arrived to assure victory. God's provision today is his Holy Spirit waiting to override self-wills and set the captives free.

Appendix A contains a Leader's Manual for launching *On Fire for God* groups for accountability and for training leaders to penetrate the culture.

Changing the culture will not be easy but it was not easy for the early Christians, for John Wesley, or for our Founders. The rewards, Christ's words, "well done my good and faithful servant. Matthew 25:21."

Appendix A:
Leader's Manual

On Fire for God (OFG) Groups

Blessed are the pure in heart for they shall see God. Matthew 5:8

Congratulations!

You are giving leadership to a ministry that should be basic in every church but that has been missing for a long time, a ministry of systematic and intentional *care and cure of* souls, a process also known as *spiritual cleansing* or as *sanctification.*

Deep inside, in each of our souls, a battle is going on between our image of

God nature derived in creation and our sin nature inherited from Adam and Eve after their fall in the Garden of Eden.

Importance of Spiritual Cleansing

Spiritual cleansing leads to purity and the blessings that flow from seeing God's plan more clearly. Our culture gives meticulous attention to mental and physical difficulties but much less to problems of the soul, a major reason we have moved from a spiritual to a materialistic culture.

We become what we feed on. 95% of what impacts our heart each day from cultural communications (TV, radio, internet, etc.) is blatant materialism that feeds our old nature, leaving 5% for feeding the soul. Spiritual impurity can be very addictive.

Our *soul* is the innermost part of our being. It largely controls how we think, feel, and act. The soul, like the stomach and mind, needs purity to properly function.

God's Word is a superb source of soul food but to be utilized the soul must be cleansed. Soul food can come from preaching, teaching, Bible study, Quiet Time, and discussions with believers but effective assimilation requires a clean vessel.

OFG groups were designed for spiritual cleansing. A key to your job as group leader is to stimulate and moderate the flow of discussion in the cleansing process. This requires that you provide encouragement, affirmation, suggestions, and support.

Background

You might be asked, where did the plan for OFG groups come from? The primary source is John Wesley's 18th century *Class Meetings*. Not unlike today he lived in a country (England) when spirituality was at low ebb. The "Church had drifted into trifling worldliness." There was also a wide gap between the rich and poor. Wesley took his message directly to the people. In 40 years his groups impacted the whole of England.

Other sources for OFG groups include Moravian and Quakers teachings and 12-step-programs.

Meetings

Meetings are held in homes, churches or any comfortable setting for relaxed friendship.

Start meetings promptly with a prayer and a hymn if appropriate. By starting promptly you communicate a message that the OFG process is important, the meeting is important, and that *care and cure of souls* is important. Music provides an important emotional dimension that involves the heart. Move promptly to sharing.

Sharing Personal Experiences

The primary purpose for meeting is members sharing spiritual *experiences*, especially experiences since the last meeting. The curricula each week is,

- What has God done in your life this week? and

- In what ways has there been other than absolute: honesty, gentleness, self-control, patience, love, and thoughtfulness

Intentional sharing of these experiences stimulates members to see weekly activities as God sees them, in a spiritual dimension.

Dual Role of Leader

Your role is both as a leader and as a group member in need of cleansing.

John Wesley advised,

> *"The leader needs to model by stating the condition of his or her own spiritual life along with stories concerning the previous week's experience, thanking God for progress and honestly sharing any failures, sins, temptations, griefs, or inner battles."*

See each member as a gift from God in need of cleansing but also one who will provide insights and affirmation for others. Members stimulate spiritual cleansing in one another.

Your strongest help in leading will be to communicate a loving attitude flowing from the knowledge that we are all fallen but all precious in God's eyes.

Confidentiality

Confidentiality must be observed at all times. A reminder of this from time to time is appropriate.

Group Make-up

Eight to twelve members is a good number for a group. A heterogenous mix including age, sex, occupation, and spiritual readiness provides rich resources for helping one another.

A three-month minimum commitment is a good target for a new OFG ministry. Many members will want to continue beyond that. Wesley found some groups and members stayed together for several years.

Qualifications

Who is ready for a group? Since everyone has dross in their life, readiness can include anyone from *seeker* to *mature* believer who recognizes the need for spiritual cleansing.

The primary qualification for admission is a desire to see God's plan for their life more clearly.

Visitors

Groups need to maintain a solid core but they also need to be open to visitors. Normally newcomers will make two visits before being considered for group membership. Once a member of a group individuals are expected to remain for at least three months.

When a group begins to exceed fourteen in number consider splitting into two groups.

Curricula

Members are expected to study the Bible during the week, either individually or in a group. Start each meeting by asking members what God is doing in their lives. That question is the curricula each week.

The emphasis in OFG groups is cleansing hearts to help members both know and do God's will. Helping members live out the word has often been a neglected ministry.

Interactive Discussion

The leader starts each meeting by sharing what God has done in his/her life the previous week. Then ask members with the same question.

Members should not feel pressure to share but observant leaders will develop the ability to identify facial and body language that indicates a desire to contribute. Responses from quiet members can result in some of the most significant break-throughs.

Pauses in discussions are normal and a not unhealthy part of the process. A pause provides time for the Holy Spirit to search and convict. A pause may seem awkward but that is partly because we often neglect to include time for the Holy Spirit to participate in discussions.

You will gradually learn when to break silence with a discussion question and what questions are appropriate for members of your group. There will be times where twenty or thirty second pauses will aid in re-focusing on the purpose of the meeting—spiritual cleansing.

Sharing spiritual experiences is a superb way to stimulate spiritual growth. However members who initiate a concern need to understand they need to arrive at decisions themselves. Others can share similar experiences and tell what worked for them but refrain from, "Here is what you ought to do."

Repentance

Cleansing souls involves *identifying* and *repenting* of thoughts, words, and deeds that do not glorify God. *Identifying* is normally painless but sincere *repentance* can involve sorrow and remorse, an uncomfortable apology, and sometimes restitution.

While members may need help from other group members to determine appropriate acts of repentance the follow-up commitment and final decision

80

should come from the member who revealed the need.

Sensitive Matters

The changes needed for the *care and
cure of souls* are "common to man." As
members begin to understand this, they
will be more willing to share experiences.
However some experiences involve "intimate details" that lead to discomfort
that can block the free flow of discussion. What is considered "intimate" may
vary greatly even from group to group
depending on the individuals in the
group.

If there is a question of sensitivity the
leader should consider changing the
venue for the discussion from the group
to a one-on-one discussion at a later
time with the individual or individuals
involved.

Higher Power

Keep the discussion on personal spiritual experiences but recognize there will be times to discuss Holy Spirit power. Some members will need to know how they can have this power. If there is any question of whether a member has experienced the indwelling spirit suggest they;

- *Talk* to God. Tell Him you need help.

- *Repent* of sins you are aware of and give them to Him.

- *Claim* Revelation 3:20.

- *Ask* the Holy Spirit to take over your life and make you the person you were meant to be.

- *Thank* God for sending His son to die for your sins that you might have life abundant and everlasting.

The enemy is especially threatened when dealing with matters of the soul. Expect resistance but recognize Holy Spirit power in a cleansed heart will prevail, "the one who is in you is greater than the one who is in the world." (1 John 4:4b)

Church Growth

OFG groups are a natural for church growth. As members experience victory in their battles against the enemy they "cannot help speaking about what we have seen and heard" Acts 4:20, and they will want to invite others to the OFG group.

Remind members OFG groups are designed to reproduce. This was the great secret of John Wesley's ministry.

If visitors are connected with another church body encourage them to maintain that connection and start an OFG

group in their church. Wesley's slogan
sums up the goal, "To spread scriptural
holiness throughout the land."

Supplement

Leading an OFG group is an opportunity to be used by God to "release the captives from bondage." Let members know, as The Living Bible translates one passage, "We are rotten through and through." OFG is designed to get rid of rot.

OFG leadership is a challenge but a rewarding opportunity to spend meaningful and precious hours growing in Christ to be used by God in changing our nation.

Suggested process:

1. Bonding time. Open with a song and a prayer.

2. Share what God has been doing in your soul this week.

3. Invite others to do the same.

4. Provide encouragement.

5. Contact and encourage members during the week.

6. Emphasize the importance of good soul food through Bible reading, worship, prayer, and daily quiet time.

7. Encourage members to live biblically, especially by loving God and loving neighbors.

Two simple tests are helpful to identify whether our thoughts, words, or deeds are part of God's plan or from the enemy:

1. What does the *Bible* say?

2. Does the thought, word, or deed *glorify* God?

The Stakes are High

When leading an *On Fire for God* group you are joining with Christ in carrying out His ministry.

- Christ said, "I came to cast fire upon the earth." (Luke 12:49)

- He also said, "I am the vine; you are the branches. If you remain in me and I in you, you will bear much fruit;" (John 15:5) OFG is designed to bear much fruit.

- "America has turned away from God, and its only hope is that it returns to God." (Rabbi Cahn, Decision magazine, March 21, 2021, p. 11)

- "Blessed is the nation whose God is the Lord." (Psalm 33:12)

OFG Discussion Questions

1. What *help* did you gain from this Group this past week?

2. Is it *hard* in this Group for you to talk about God in your life?

3. What *new insights* about yourself did you gain this week?

4. Did you experience *joy* in your life in a new and special way?

5. What did you do to find *peace?*

6. Any *worries* this past week? Did you sense God's presence?

7. What *spiritual changes* in your life you would like to make?

8. Any *new understandings* about God this week?

9. Was there *stress* in your life that was a problem? How did you handle it?

10. Are you reading any *books* that help you grow spiritually?

11. Was there a time this week where you experienced *special peace* with God?

12. Any situations that led you to *feel* especially bad or good about yourself?

13. Did you experience God's *forgiveness* in a new way this week?

14. Are you reaching out to *love neighbors*? Any missed opportunities?

15. When did you feel *closest to God* this week?

16. Have you felt you were *growing spiritually*, or felt you needed to grow spiritually?

17. Was there a time you especially sensed the *Holy Spirit's* presence?

18. Are you growing spiritually? If so what *triggered the growth*?

As you feel led, rephrase these questions to keep the focus on recent personal experiences involving God, the fruit of the Spirit, loving God and neighbors, etc.

About the Author

Jim Dickson, an Army veteran with degrees in political science, history, and law, served churches in the U.S. and Eastern Europe in discipleship and evangelism for over 35 years. Jim writes on human nature, God's provisions, the faith of America's Founding Fathers, spiritual values, and obedience to God's Word. Jim

and his wife Peggy have five children and numerous grand and great
grandchildren.